ROYAL TOURS
OF THE BRITISH EMPIRE
1860–1927

— I —

EDWARD, PRINCE OF WALES, AT GOVERNMENT HOUSE, CHARLOTTETOWN,
1860.
The Prince had landed at St John's, Newfoundland, on 23 July at the
start of his North American tour, the first to be made by the heir to
the Throne. The Prince stands third from the right leaning on his
sword. In the centre is the Governor of Novia Scotia and his wife, the
Earl and Countess of Mulgrave, heir to the Marquis of Normanby.
Between the Countess and the Prince stands the Duke of Newcastle,
Secretary to the Colonies who accompanied the Prince of Wales on this
tour.

ROYAL TOURS

OF THE
BRITISH EMPIRE
1860–1927

JOHN FABB

B.T. BATSFORD LTD, LONDON

ISBN 0 7134 5205 6

BOOK DESIGN BY ALAN HAMP
TYPESET BY SERVIS FILMSETTING LTD, MANCHESTER
AND PRINTED IN GREAT BRITAIN BY
BUTLER AND TANNER, FROME
SOMERSET
FOR THE PUBLISHERS B.T. BATSFORD LTD
4 FITZHARDINGE STREET,
LONDON W1H OAH

INTRODUCTION

Nowadays the visit of a member of the Royal family to a part of the Commonwealth is a common occurence. In a matter of hours, the destination is reached and often the visit concluded. The member of the Royal family then returns in relative comfort and speed to Great Britain. In the Victorian period, however, visits to the Empire had to be carefully arranged and travel detail meticulously worked out. The difficulties were daunting: usually weeks at sea and then travel by train, or more exotic means of travel depending on the part of the Empire to be toured.

Queen Victoria did not travel to her Empire; even her visits to France and Germany were infrequent and became more so as the Queen grew older, especially after the death of Prince Albert. To travel to the outposts of the empire was a new venture as the Napoleonic Wars, followed by the reigns of two elderly kings, had made such journeys difficult and improbable. In addition, Queen Victoria had nine children who needed their mother's attention, and her frequent pregnancies made such visits impracticable. The death of Prince Albert in 1861, followed by over 20 years' mourning made any empire journeys by the Queen unlikely.

This did not stop, however, the Queen's interest in her ever expanding Empire, and her family was able to make the visits in her name. Albums of photographs were taken at the time, although mainly of views and not of the Princes and Princesses who undertook these trips. The photographs were, of course, the first glimpse that Queen Victoria had of her Empire and views of famous and historical sites would have been of great interest to her and other members of the Royal family back home.

When Queen Victoria's proclamation was read on 1 November 1858 to the Princes of India, transferring the authority of the East India Company to the Crown, it was hoped that a Royal tour might be arranged. The Prince of Wales was 17 at the time and it was in the scheme of instruction and education of Prince Albert that his sons, and in particular the heir apparent, should visit the Empire. However, the political climate was such that a tour of India was postponed until a later date. Eventually, it was Prince Alfred, the Duke of Edinburgh and second son of the Queen, who was the first member of the Royal family to set foot in India, when his ship briefly visited Bombay and other ports in 1860.

Canada and the United States of America, 1869

At the end of the Crimean War in 1856, a deputation of representatives from Canada came to England and asked if Her Majesty would pay a visit to their country. Victoria declined, but suggested that the Prince of Wales (later, Edward VII) might go in the near future. In 1860 it was decided that the Prince would cross the Atlantic and perform the opening ceremony of the Victoria Tubular Bridge which crossed the St Lawrence River and was considered an engineering triumph of the age. The Prince would also lay the foundation stone of the Parliamentary Building to be erected in Ottawa, the capital of the Dominion of Canada. When the United States of America learned of the planned trip, President Buchan approached Queen Victoria to see if the Prince could be allowed to visit Washington, where he was assured of a great welcome. The Queen and Her Government replied that such a visit would give the Prince great pleasure and that he looked forward to meeting President Buchan in person.

The Prince and his suite left in July 1860 on board the battleship *Hero*, together with a squadron of smaller warships; they reached St John's Newfoundland on 23 July for a two day visit. Four days later the squadron sailed into Halifax, Novia Scotia, where the Prince received a tumultuous welcome, having been accompanied along part of the way by Red Indians in their birch bark canoes. Banquets, a review of the garrison troops, and a regatta made up the days spent there before the Royal party left by steam train for Windsor and Houseport. Rejoining the warships they made their way up the St Lawrence River to Quebec and here, too, the welcome was overwhelming. The Prince then held a levée after the opening of the two houses of the Canadian Parliament. It was on this occasion that the Prince personally conferred the honour of Knighthood in the Queen's name on the speakers of the upper and lower houses of the Canadian Parliament. Five days later the journey was continued up river to Montreal, where 40,000 people waited to catch a glimpse of the Prince. Again there was the usual round of meetings with politicians, clergy, and the army that was all part of a Royal visit. A large body of Red Indians also met the Prince and then accompanied him to the great railway bridge across the St Lawrence River that he had officially come to open (*fig. 3*). Then on to Ottawa, where the Prince laid the foundation stone of the Houses of Parliament. This first State Visit was a complete success; the crowds continually insisted that the Prince show himself again and again at windows and railcar verandas. The Government at home was delighted and it set the seal on future tours abroad for the British Royal family.

The Prince of Wales had not, however, finished with North American continent for there was the promised visit to the United States of America. The Royal party left Canadian soil at Windsor and journeyed by train to Detroit. Over 30,000 people were waiting to catch a glimpse of the Royal visitor, and because of the large crowd it was impossible to move the carriages for some time. At the hotel where the Royal suite was staying, vast crowds converged and waited until midnight hoping to see the Prince. The next day the Prince continued to Chicago, where an even larger crowd, estimated at some 150,000 people, waited to see him arrive. Luckily the Royal party was able to rest at last and recuperate from the fatigue of the last few weeks. They slipped away to a quiet little town called Dwight, where the Prince spent a few days out on the prairie, riding and shooting game. The Royal party continued down the Mississippi River by steamer to St Louis, and then by train to Cincinnati, always being welcomed by the enthusiatic and friendly American crowds. Pittsburg and Harrisburg were two more whistle stops along the way to Washington. At the station a more formal meeting took place between the President and the Prince of Wales, together with the Prince's suite and members of the American Government. Thousands of people lined the route to the White House and a state banquet that night ended a busy and historic day for the Prince. Some days of entertainment and touring historic sights followed, which ended at the tomb of George Washington, who had defeated the army of the Prince's great-grandfather and thus brought into being the United States of America. At New York the Prince in his scarlet uniform of a Colonel in the British Army cantered his horse down to the battery where he inspected the volunteer troops of the New York State. A ball followed that evening and the Prince danced with pretty American socialites until five in the morning. Next, the Prince went to Boston where he met a survivor of the historic battle of Bunker Hill who had fought through most of the American War of Independence. The Prince and his suite rejoined the battleship *Hero* at Boston and together with the other warships steamed home to a grateful government and a hero's welcome from the British people. At Windsor the Prince was received by his mother and family, all eager to hear of that memorable first Royal tour. It is unfortunate that few photographs appear to have survived – if indeed any were taken on the tour – apart from some formal groups at Washington and New York.

AUSTRALIA AND NEW ZEALAND, 1867 TO 1869

IN 1868 QUEEN VICTORIA'S second son, Prince Alfred, Duke of Edinburgh, spent a seven month voyage on his ship *HMS Galatea* (of which he was captain) touring Australia and New Zealand (*fig. 8*). Landing in South Australia he was able to hunt Kangaroos as well as receive the crowds of eager colonists. Adelaide and Sydney were included in the tour as well as Hobart in Tasmania. In Sydney, however, the Prince was shot at and slightly wounded by a would-be assassin named O'Farrell. The Prince had been at a picnic where he was due to present a cheque for charity. Fortunately, Florence Nightingale had just sent out two trained nurses to work at the Sydney Hospital and in their capable hands the Prince recovered, although the tour was delayed. O'Farrell paid the full penalty of the law and was hanged.

In 1869 Prince Alfred journeyed on board his ship to New Zealand, the first Royal visitor to those islands. He arrived at Auckland on 10 May and was met by three large war canoes manned by 200 loyal tribesmen, who had paddled out with their chiefs, singing and chanting their welcome. The guns of *HMS Galatea* fired a salute, which was replied to by the battery of the Royal Naval volunteers on shore. The Prince landed wearing civilian clothing to the tumultuous cheers of the large crowd assembled. To celebrate his arrival triumphal arches were erected, decorated with New Zealand ferns and shrubs, and photographs were taken to show these decorations (*fig. 14*). The Governor of New Zealand presented various dignitaries including the Maori Chief Orakei. A carriage drive through the city streets brought the Prince to Government House where he held a levée and received a deputation of Maori Chiefs who brought gifts of mats, weapons and cloth for himself and Queen Victoria. On 24 May the Queen's birthday ball was held, followed by further public engagements. The Duke then left with his naval squadron for the Sandwich Islands, whose inhabitants were anxious to be annexed by the British Crown. These Islands are now known as the Hawaiian Islands and are part of the United States of America.

CANADA, 1869 AND 1870

IN 1869 PRINCE ARTHUR, third son of Queen Victoria, visited Canada. He was a lieutenant in the Royal Engineers and 19 years old. Canada welcomed him with enthusiasm. He made a long tour in Upper Canada hunting and shooting. He also met the chiefs of the six nations of the Indian tribe confederation and was himself invested as an Indian Chief. Banquets and balls followed on his return to civilization. In particular, he was given a hearty welcome on his arrival at Quebec. He followed his brother, the Prince of Wales, in visiting the United States and was received by the President and the people with their usual boisterous welcome.

THE FAR EAST, 1869

AT THE SAME TIME Prince Alfred, Duke of Edinburgh, was in the colony of Hong Kong, on the first Royal visit to that country. From there the Prince proceeded to Malaya and then Calcutta in India where he was given a splendid welcome by the Indian Princes. Sixty elephants were in the procession to Government House where the Prince held a durbar for the Indian rulers. He continued his tour by visiting Ceylon (now Sri Lanka) in May 1870, where he was fêted by the local people, and he also made a journey into the interior for an elephant hunt. After he left Ceylon he visited the island of Mauritius and then Cape Town before returning to England.

INDIA, 1875

IN 1875 OCCURRED the most ambitious Royal tour ever contemplated. India had long been waiting for an official visit by the Queen's eldest son, Albert Edward, the Prince of Wales – later Edward VII. Negotiations took place between the two Governments, and eventually it was announced that the Prince would visit India during the winter months of 1875 and that the Government of India would pay all expenses. The Prince and his party departed on 11 October 1875, to Dover and then on to Paris, pausing briefly for lunch with the President of the new Republic of France. They continued by train to Brindisi in Italy where *HMS Serapis* lay with her escort of warships. The ships then passed through the Suez Canal and out into the Red Sea. The voyage across the Indian Ocean was uneventful except for occasional breakdown of the steam machinery.

On 8 November the city of Bombay was plainly visible to the Royal party on the deck of the *Serapis*. The Viceroy, Lord Northbrook, welcomed the Prince of Wales on reaching India, and preparations were made to land (*fig. 22*). Eagerly awaiting the Prince while sitting on long lines of benches draped in scarlet cloth were Rajahs, Maharajahs, Chiefs, Sirdars and gentlemen of the Presidency of Bombay Province, Hindus, Mahrattas and Muhamadans. It was a crowd glittering with gems as they waited for a sight of the Royal visitor. Massed sweet smelling flowers were arranged around the landing stage. A great shout went up as the Prince of Wales stepped on to Indian soil; the troops presented arms, and the massed bands broke into *God save the Queen*. After receiving assurances of their devotion to the Throne of England and addresses of welcome, the future Emperor of India met the Indian Princes personally. In the evening there was a state ball and reception. The Prince's birthday, on 9 November, was an event that was celebrated all over India. A Durbar was held in accordance with court etiquette for the Princes of the Bombay Presidency. The Prince of Wales wore the uniform of a Field Marshal and was attended by his whole suite in full dress uniform and decorations. Each Indian Prince was received separately with all due ceremony. The Prince of Wales sat on a throne of solid silver and after compliments had been exchanged the Political Officer led the Indian Princes to the chairs set apart for them. Here for the first time the Prince of Wales was able to see the magnificence and the fabulous wealth of the Indian Princes. The Maharajah of Kolhapur, a boy of 12, was dressed in blue velvet encrusted with diamonds, his turban strung with rubies. The Maharajah of Mysore wore a necklace of untold value, each stone the size of a pigeon's egg, his neck, wrists, and ankles encircled with strings of pearls, rubies and diamonds. The Maharajah of Udaipur, a fierce warrior, wore a belt made of gold, set with rubies, from which hung his sword; the hilt was of gold enamel encrusted with rubies. The Rao of Cutch, a portly old man who rose from his sick bed to pay homage to the Prince, returned to his state to die, his duty done. Another Young Prince of 12 years was the Gaekwar of Baroda, and because of his brilliant costume covered in jewels, the Prince's suite described him as a crystallized rainbow. Rajahs were followed by Nabobs, followed in their turn by Dewans and Maharajahs until all had been presented. Each ruler had given the Prince of Wales a costly gift of jewels, weapons and armour, worth a king's ransom and still in the possession of the Royal family. The day ended with a state banquet.

The next day the Prince met 7000 children at a fête and was regaled with songs and nearly smothered in flowers. After further receptions and reviews the Prince and his party departed by train on a visit to the young Gaekwar of Baroda. On arrival at the border the Royal party was received by the young ruler and his ministers, accompanied by a crowd of tens of thousands who had come to see the future Emperor of India. The usual durbar allowed the Gaekwar to introduce Prince Albert Edward to his Sirdars. Later the Prince was entertained by a combat between two elephants, who wrestled together over a low wall as well as hitting each other with their trunks. Later the Prince and his suite were allowed a few days' shooting and then returned to the Royal Yacht for the voyage to Ceylon. The reception at Colombo, was a repetition of those on the mainland, and the next day the Prince moved inland to Kandy. Ceremonial receptions were arranged for meetings with the chiefs and their wives as well as the conferring of knighthoods and honours to the Colonial Government civil servants. The next few days were spent hunting elephants in the interior jungle and the Prince managed to shoot one during a torrential downpour of tropical rain. The Royal party then returned to Colombo and the Royal Yacht. That night the squadron slipped its moorings and steamed up the coast towards Madras. The city was reached by steam train after the Prince had landed at Tuticorin. The thousands of people who greeted the Prince here followed his every movement, but the Prince managed to get away to a meeting of the Madras pack of hounds at Guindy Park where, after a run of nine miles, a Jackal was killed.

From Madras the journey continued to Calcutta, the capital of India. The receptions were most impressive and included one for the Indian Princes at Government House. The Prince received the Maharajah of Patiala and the Maharajah Holkar of Indore. A wealth of gems covered their bodies and they arrived in carriages drawn by four, gold-harnessed, pure white arab horses. The Maharajah of Kashmir and Jammu and the Maharajah of Gwalior followed resplendent in Indian silks, their turbans decorated with diamonds, rubies, and sapphires. The Prince was also introduced to the Begum of Bhopal whose country was traditionally ruled by the matriarchal line of the Royal family. The last

Prince introduced was the Maharajah of Rewah who, in common with the other Princes, presented the Prince of Wales with costly tribute.

Christmas was spent in the traditional manner with the Viceroy and his family and friends; it included entertainments on board the Royal Yacht. On New Year's Day a chapter of the Order of the Star of India was held. Huge tents were erected in the grounds of Government House decorated with carpets, gold cloth and the Royal Coat of Arms. The Prince of Wales sat on a silver throne beneath a canopy of sky blue silk held up by silver pillars. A salvo of artillery preceded the magnificent pageant as the Indian Princes entered the tent dressed not only in Eastern finery but also the robes of the Order of the Star of India. The Maharajah of Jodhpur was elevated to the Order, as was the Rajah of Jind; the Maharajah of Panna was invested with the Order of Knight Commander. The Prince of Wales and his party then went to the City of Benares (now called Voranasi), and then on to the ancient capital, Delhi, for a grand review of the army. Everywhere the Prince was entertained lavishly and showered with costly jewels and gifts by the rulers of the Indian states. The cities of Lahore and Kashmir followed with more durbars and, for light relief, a little polo and hunting. The best hunting enjoyed by Prince Edward was found in the foothills of the Himalayas and Nepal where he and his party bagged considerable trophies before returning to Bombay and the Royal Yacht.

On 13 March the Prince of Wales left India for the return journey to England. The tour had covered 7000 miles by land and over 2000 by sea. After a stop at Malta the ships steamed on to Yarmouth. Here the Royal Yacht slowed down to allow the Princess of Wales, accompanied by her children, to board for a private reunion with her husband. The Royal party disembarked at Portsmouth on 12 May 1876.

THE WORLD TOUR, 1879 TO 1882

IN THE SUMMER of 1879, the two sons of the Prince of Wales, Prince Albert Victor and Prince George (later George V), were sent on a world tour. This was to last, with one break at home, three years, until 1882 – an ambitious programme. Prince Albert Victor was 15 and Prince George 14. Both were Royal Naval cadets and had joined HMS Bacchante after completing their course on the Britannia. The Prince of Wales had decided that a first hand knowledge of the British Empire was more important than visiting European courts. The health of Prince Albert Victor was also beginning to be a cause for concern, and it was thought that a sea voyage would be good for him. HMS Bacchante was a fast armoured cruiser using both sail and steam, weighing just over 4000 tons, with a crew of 450 men. Not only did the two Princes carry out their naval duties but they also had to attend lessons under a resident tutor. Gibraltar was the first port of call and then they went across the Atlantic to the British West Indies. At Bridgetown, Barbados, a great welcome was given to the Princes and again at Trinidad where they were allowed to wear the uniform of midshipmen having received their commissions (*fig. 25*). Granada came next, then Union Island, St Vincent, Martinique, Dominica, St Thomas and Jamaica. They reached Bermuda on 29 March 1880 in stormy weather. A fortnight was spent here on routine naval instructions as well as ceremonial visits. *HMS Bacchante* then set sail for England and a family reunion at Portsmouth. It was on this voyage that Prince George decided that he wanted to make the Royal Navy his career.

On 14 September 1880 the two Princes left once more on *HMS Bacchante* for the South Atlantic and the Falkland Islands with its few white settlers and some Indian tribesmen. At the time there was talk of exchanging with France the Island of New Caledonia in the Pacific for the Falkland Islands but the proposal came to nothing. In February, Cape Town in South Africa was reached. The Boers in the Transvaal were in rebellion and there was ill feeling in pro-Boer Cape Town towards the Royal visitors. No welcoming crowds were seen and Dutch flags were hoisted to show the anti-British feeling. The Governor did his best to entertain the boys, and they had an agreeable time. One of their more interesting experiences was a visit to Cetewayo, the King of Zululand, who had been deposed in 1879 after the Zulu War and was now on a farm near Cape Town.

The squadron left Simonstown and set sail for Australia where after severe storms the *Bacchante* without her steering gear, steamed into Albany, Western Australia. Here there was a rousing welcome from this small town and they were able to stay on a farm with one of the settlers while the ship was being repaired. Owing to this mishap the Princes travelled by Royal Mail steamer to Adelaide, where they received a huge welcome, and then on to Melbourne. A huge ball was given in their honour with all the government and society of the colony present. In complete contrast the two Princes were allowed to go down the shaft of a gold mine, much to their excitement (*fig. 26*). At least 2000 people greeted them at Sandhurst, South Australia, and they were provided with an escort of the Prince of Wales light horse cavalry and accompanied by the Highland pipers. Here, again, there were gold mines to be seen and a great ball in the evening. The repair work to the *Bacchante* made the stay in New South Wales longer than expected, but the Governor, mindful of the boys' youth, made sure they had plenty of leisure time for horseback riding and tennis. After a tour of the city of Sydney, where the people turned out in force to see Queen Victoria's grandsons, *HMS Bacchante* steamed out on 20 August 1881 for the island of Fiji.

In Fiji the Princes were received by King Thakombau who was especially noted for his ferocity. He had clubbed a boy to death when he was only six and had strangled five of his father's wives when they had stood in his way to the throne. He greeted the two Princes with full ceremony by the drinking of Kava mixed in a great wooden bowl strained and served in coconuts. The King's eldest son served the the Princes and the Governor. Sixteen oxen were roasted and eaten, together with a variety of tropical fruits. Afterwards, there was native dancing and the presentation of a whale's tooth to Prince Albert Victor (*fig. 28*). The next port of call was Japan, a new country to western nations as it had previously been barred from trade and travel. The Princes were disappointed that the dress of the Imperial Court was European and that the Emperor wore the uniform of a Field Marshal. Hong Kong and Singapore were followed by Ceylon. The two Princes were greatly excited by the round up of wild elephants that they attended. Aden and the Suez Canal brought the squadron into the Mediterranean, but not before the two Princes had climbed to the top of one of the pyramids in Egypt.

INDIA, 1889

IN 1889 IT WAS DECIDED that Prince Albert Victor, Duke of Clarence and Avondale, should visit India. As the eldest son of the Prince of Wales, he was in direct descent to succeed to the throne of the British Empire and consequently would become Emperor of India. The Prince had also fallen in love with Princess Alexandra of Hesse and the Rhine, a dazzling beauty who had spurned him and become engaged instead to the heir to the Imperial throne of Russia – Crown Prince Nicholas. It was hoped that the visit to India would allow the Prince to get over this affair of the heart, which was a regular occurrence as the Prince had fallen in and out of love with many Princesses. He arrived in Bombay to a great welcome from the people and in solemn state by the ruling Princes of India. He travelled across India to the capital, Calcutta, and was received by the Viceroy. He then visited the Indian army at Muridke (*fig. 31*) which was under the command of Lieutenant General Sir Frederick Roberts, Commander in Chief of the Indian Army. The Prince then returned to Bombay for passage back to Great Britain.

THE WORLD TOUR, 1901

WITH THE DEATH of Prince Albert Victor, Duke of Clarence and Avondale, in 1891, Prince George became heir to the throne after his father, the future Edward VII. He married Princess Mary of Teck in 1893, and in 1901 Prince George, now Duke of Cornwall and York, together with the Duchess, set out on a tour of the dominions to develop closer relations between those countries and the crown. Twenty-two years had passed since the Duke had visited any part of the Empire in an official capacity. Australia had requested that the Duke and Duchess visit the newly formed federation and open the first session of the Parliament. New Zealand had also renewed an invitation through their Governor. The death of Queen Victoria threatened the tour, but on the insistence of the King Edward VII the tour went ahead. Delay would have made the tour impossible for some time, as the Duke had to be in London for his father's coronation. On 16 March 1901 the *Ophir*, an Orient steam ship company liner converted to a Royal yacht, steamed out. Gibraltar and Malta were again the first ports of call, and the yacht continued through the Suez Canal to Aden and then Ceylon where the Royal couple met Arabi Pasha, the exiled Egyptian general defeated in the war of 1881. He asked the Duke to intercede on his behalf for his return to Egypt after 19 years in exile; shortly afterwards Arabi Pasha was released. At Singapore homage was paid by the Sultans of the recently federated states of Malaya, and later the Duchess received the Sultanas in private audience. On 5 May 1901, *Ophir* steamed into Port Melbourne a day ahead of schedule, but the Royal party waited until the next day before disembarking. Vessels of the Australian squadron as well as foreign warships lay at anchor in the harbour. Bands played and each ship fired a salute as the *Ophir* steamed past. The Prime Minister of Australia welcomed the Duke and Duchess and a carriage procession, complete with an escort drawn form the Australian forces, drove through the crowded streets. A state banquet, followed by a day of rest, preceded the day chosen for the opening of Parliament. Enormous crowds packed the streets long before the Duke and Duchess appeared in their open carriage. At the ceremonial opening of Parliament the Duke and Duchess faced the senators of the new Parliament; behind them sat the Governors of the six Australian States. Between 12,000 and 15,000 people had been arranged down the vast aisles. The next few days were filled with celebrations including a military review on Flemington Race Course and, more unusually, a parade of over 10,000 cheering Trade Unionists. The Royal couple then travelled to the gold mines at Ballarat, but this time the Duke did not attempt to go down the mine as he had done with his brother many years previously. A train journey of over 1000 miles brought them to Brisbane in Queensland and another enthusiastic welcome. Here, too, were Aborigines carrying spears decorated with emu feathers; displays of dancing were performed and gifts presented (*fig. 35*). A week was spent in Sydney; two events were of special importance: the presentation of medals to the officers and men of the New South Wales contingent who had returned from the Boer War, and a demonstration by 20,000 school children who sang in front of an estimated audience of 130,000 people.

New Zealand was the next port of call. In Auckland the Maoris made a special welcome to the Duke and Duchess with traditional dances and gifts. Wellington, Christchurch, and Dunedin tried to outdo each other with the fervour of their welcome (*fig. 39*). The Duke sent a letter to the Governor telling him of the delightful and unforgetable impression he would always have of New Zealand. *Ophir* then steamed back towards Australia and made a short stay in Tasmania (*see fig. 49*). This was then a sparsely populated island, but nevertheless nearly 600 men from Tasmania had fought in the Boer War and two soldiers had won the Victoria Cross. The Royal yacht steamed on to Adelaide in South

Australia and then to Albany where a train journey took the party to Perth. Here, the Royal couple said farewell to Australia, and thousands of people packed the wharfs or secured places on the small ships and vessels in the harbour to see *Ophir* steam out to the Island of Mauritius. From there South Africa was next and, in particular, Pietermaritzburg. Here among the passions raised by the Boers there was a strong police presence but the enthusiastic welcome was overwhelming. Simonstown and Cape Town completed the tour. *Ophir* then steamed up the coast of Africa and across the Atlantic for the next phase of the Royal tour – Canada.

Quebec was reached on 16 September 1901. The time chosen for the Royal visit was a delightful one as far as the weather was concerned as Canada is seen at its best during the weeks of autumn. The rich red of the maple leaves and the colourful tints of the foliage make an unforgettable spectacle. Travel was by the Canadian Pacific Railway and Quebec was the starting point. Here the Royal couple received a special deputation from the French Canadians, who expressed their loyalty to the throne. In its turn, Montreal demonstrated its enthusiasm for the Duke and Duchess, as did Ottawa, the capital city. They continued to Calgary where they were given a spectacular welcome by the Red Indians (*fig. 58*). The Duke, dressed in military uniform received a dense mass of varied Canadian tribes and their chiefs. The tour continued towards Vancouver over the Rocky Mountains. On the return journey at Banff the Duke did a little shooting, and the tour resumed in Montreal's rival for the capital of Canada, Toronto, which gave the Royal couple their finest reception of the whole tour and vast crowds surpassed all that had gone before. The Duke reviewed 10,000 troops, and a state reception was the highlight of their stay in that city. Niagara Falls Hamilton, Halifax, and Novia Scotia (*fig. 64*) were the last places to receive the Royal party before *Ophir* steamed out towards Portsmouth and England, which she reached on 31 October 1901.

INDIA, 1905 AND 1906

IN 1905 A TOUR of the Indian Empire was made by George, Prince of Wales, who was accompanied by Mary, Princess of Wales; their children were left in the care of Edward VII. The voyage was made on *HMS Renown*, and facilities were made for the daily press to send special correspondence to accompany the tour. Intelligence was sent and received by the novel method of wireless telegraphy. The Royal party landed at Bombay (*fig. 65*) and the occasion was of great magnificence. Maharajahs and Princes of the Bombay Presidency had come in their most gorgeous robes of vived coloured silks, decked with many costly jewels, to greet their Emperor's son and heir. The Prince and Princess were greeted by the Viceroy, Lord Curzon, and Lady Curzon. A state reception attended by 4000 people started the festivities, which lasted one week in Bombay. The most important event was the reception of the ten leading chiefs of the Bombay Presidency at Government House. Everything possible was done to add dignity to the occasion. On arrival each native Prince was met with a guard of honour and a salute of artillery in accordance with his rank. Then came the presentation of the *Nazar*, or tribute, from the Indian Princes and their retainers. The *Nazar* was a number of golden mohurs in a silk purse varying according to rank and it was touched and remitted by Prince George. At Indore, one of the first cities of the native states to be visited, 20 Princes were in attendance to greet the Royal visitors. Udaipur, city of the Rajput warrior race of India, welcomed the Royal couple with the walls, palace front, and houses glowing with thousands of lights made from earthenware saucers filled with oil and cotton threads. Jaipur gave the Prince a medieval reception. The Maharajah came in a carriage covered in a gold canopy, laid his sword at the Prince's feet, and swore fealty to the Emperor and his son. The two mile drive to the palace was thronged with troops, retainers and hundreds of horsemen with swords and rifles, patiently waiting to pay obeisance to the Emperor's son. State elephants fitted with brass cannon and camels with swivel blunderbusses fixed to their saddles waited to pay homage while war horns wailed and guns saluted. Bikaner, the next call, was a place for rest before the exhausting tour was resumed. The Royal group continued to Lahore and the Punjab for a durbar with the local Maharajah and his chiefs and then on to the north west frontier, furthest point of the Indian Empire. A mighty military review was held at Rawalpindi; 100,000 soldiers were gathered there under the command of Lord Kitchener, the Commander in Chief. A reception with the Maharajah of Kashmir and Jammu followed, and then the tour continued to Amritsar, city of the Sikhs. Delhi followed, which had now become a commercial city without the charm it had in the days of previous royal visits. Next, they visited Agra and the Taj Mahal, which was thought by the Princess of Wales to be the most romantic monument in all India. At Gwalior the procession to the Maharajah's palace took place on 36 elephants with howdahs of gold and silver mounted on their backs (*fig. 70*). The elephants were decorated with gold and silver chains around their necks. A banquet and a military review followed. Christmas was spent as guests of the Maharajah; the Prince and his host attended a tiger shoot in the morning and in the evening there was a splendid Christmas tree in the palace hall where the Princess of Wales gave out presents to the Royal family of Gwalior. Calcutta, then the capital of India, was overwhelmed with a sea of people hoping to see the Prince and Princess. The Royal couple then embarked for a journey by sea across the Bay of Bengal to Burma. Landing at Rangoon the Royal party visited Mandalay in Upper Burma, before departing by sea for the great city of Madras in Southern India. At Mysore the Prince and Princess were back in an Indian state ruled by a Maharajah, who had initiated many useful educational and medical reforms to bring his country up to a high standard. Hyderabad was the largest state in India, as big as

France in size, and was ruled by a Muslim Prince. Here the Prince of Wales was able to indulge in some big game hunting for tiger (*fig. 75*). After a pleasant rest with the Nizam and his family it was on to Benares in central India, somewhat spoilt by heavy rains. A big game shoot arranged by the Maharajah of Nepal had to be abandoned because of an outbreak of cholera among the people of the camp, but the Prince was able to return to Gwalior, where his friend the Maharajah arranged a little more game shooting for his honoured guest. Karachi, the last place on the tour was eventually reached, and from there the Royal party departed for England.

CANADA, 1908

IN 1908 THE PRINCE OF WALES attended a great festival in Canada to celebrate the tercentenary of Quebec which was founded in 1608 by Samuel de Champlain. The Governor General with considerable foresight had suggested that the nation purchase the Plains of Abraham, the site of General Wolfe's victory over the French. He also suggested the purchase of the field of the Battle of Sainte Foy (A French victory). Canadians of both British and French descent were satisfied. The Prince of Wales travelled to Canada in the new armoured cruiser *Indomitable*, the fastest cruiser afloat. Across the Atlantic at Quebec waited not only the British Atlantic fleet, but also French and American squadrons to greet the Prince. At Quebec the party included Count Bertrand de Montcalme, descendant of the French hero who died defending Quebec, and Mr George Wolfe, a descendant of the British General who also died on the field of battle. The speeches were given by Prince in both English and French much to the gratification of the Canadians. The occasion was a public holiday and massive crowds watched the festivities, which included a pageant of history and a military review. The Prince was attended by Field Marshal Lord Roberts and the Governor General. They watched a march of French and American sailors followed by 2,500 British sailors from the fleet. The Canadian troops who also marched in the parade were warmly congratulated by Lord Roberts on their appearance and bearing.

INDIA, 1911

IN 1910 KING EDWARD DIED and in the following year King George V decided that he would be crowned Emperor of India at Delhi. On 15 November 1911, the King and Queen left on board the latest P & O Liner, the *Medina*, (*fig. 77*) for India and their coronation durbar. Bombay, the gateway to India, was reached on 2 December and, as usual, thousands of people were there to greet them. Delhi had been chosen for the durbar because of its historical and sacred association with both Muslims and Hindus. Forty-five square miles outside the city were transformed into an actual city to accommodate the hundreds of thousands who were expected to come to witness and take part in the event. Food, sanitation and animal quarters had to be provided. It also had to be beautiful, with lawns and decorations suitable for the Emperor's coronation site. A railway was built as well as a complete telephone system, three hospitals and 52 miles of water pipes. Their Majesties arrived at Delhi in the December (*fig. 78*). At the reception pavilion the Emperor received the ruling Princes of India in audience. Then followed a review of the army; 38,000 men with 20,000 camp followers, for not only were there the British forces but also the troops of the rulers of India. Some of the soldiers wore the ancient costume of chain mail armour, while others came in modern military uniform and equipment, similar to the regular Indian army. The durbar itself took place on 12 December under a vast pavilion open on all sides so that the Emperor and Empress could be seen by everyone (*fig. 80*). An estimated 100,000 people witnessed the ceremonies that day – the last time that this ritual would be seen. In the arena were 50,000 Imperial troops and 1,600 massed bandsmen from all the regiments present. The Emperor and Empress arrived by carriage dressed in the Imperial robes and wearing the crowns of India. Seated under the huge pavilion and surrounded by their pages (who were drawn from the families of the Indian rulers) the Emperor and Empress received the homage of the Viceroy of India and his council. Then came the Princes of India and Burma in order of precedence to pay homage and swear loyalty to the throne. After this tiring and gruelling ceremony Their Majesties retired. The Emperor had also announced the transfer of his capital from Calcutta to Delhi, grants of land were given to people, certain debts were cancelled and 11,000 convicts were released from prison. Calcutta was the next city to receive Their Majesties with the thousands of people only India can muster. On 10 January 1912, two months from the day they had set out from England, the Emperor and Empress departed for home (*fig. 84*).

CANADA, 1919

THE FIRST WORLD WAR caused a disruption of Royal tours other than visits to the troops at the Front. After the end of the war, however, the Prime Minister, Lloyd George, suggested that the King might send the Prince of Wales, later Edward VIII, on a series of Royal tours that would seal the bond between Britain and the Empire. King George at once agreed. In the summer of 1919, the Prince left for Canada in the battle cruiser *HMS Renown*. After visiting Newfoundland the Prince journeyed to Quebec where he was overwhelmed by tens of thousands of people eager to see him and shake him by the hand, the first time this had occurred on a Royal tour. A parade of some 27,000 ex-servicemen broke ranks and swarmed around him, cheering and waving. Prince Edward travelled across Canada by special train and at every stop he talked to miners, farmers, and the people, reminiscing about the war and offering his condolences to the bereaved. At Ottawa he headed the Labour Day parade, and at Toronto 40,000 people broke into yells of delight when the Prince of Wales sprinted after a wounded soldier's hat and pressed it back firmly on his head. From Canada the Prince at his own request paid a short visit to the United States to a raptuous reception. President Wilson was ill in bed but insisted on seeing the Prince. At New York the welcome was all American – a snow storm of ticker tape showered down on the motorcade. He attended a magnificent ball and paid a visit to West Point Military Academy (*fig. 95*). Everywhere the Prince received a most rapturous reception.

AUSTRALIA, 1920

AFTER LESS THAN four months at home the Prince of Wales left for Australia and New Zealand, again on *HMS Renown*. As the warship passed through the Panama Canal the United States sent an aeroplane guard of honour to fly above her. The ship called in at the American base of San Diego in Southern California and at Hawaii, where a state ball was held in his honour. The Fiji Islands displayed war dances and traditional ceremonies before the Prince at last reached New Zealand. Auckland, the capital, gave him a warm reception, as did the Maoris who sang and danced before him, offering gifts and reminding the Prince of their devotion to Queen Victoria to whom they had originally sworn allegiance (*fig. 96*).

Australia was a difficult assignment for the Prince; the Prime Minister had warned him that the Australians were a tough nation and had no undue respect for Royalty and protocol. 'They must be handled with care, they hate formality', he was warned. The Prince lost no time in winning the hearts of the Australians; three quarters of a million people lined the route in Melbourne and cheered him all the way as he smiled and waved back at them. A newspaper wrote, 'He smiled away the difference which Australians believed lay between Royalty and the people'. In Sydney his welcome was even more tumultuous, and for the remainder of his visit to that country there was no doubt his appeal to the Australians (*fig. 97*). He left 'half killed by kindness', as he told the Prime Minister. The Prince returned by way of Fiji again and also Samoa; after a brief rest at Hawaii he continued through the Panama Canal for a tour of the West Indian Islands before heading home for Portsmouth.

INDIA, 1921

IN 1921, IT WAS THE TURN of the Prince of Wales to visit India again in *HMS Renown*. On arrival in Bombay, despite Ghandi's boycott, thousands of Indians lined the streets to greet the Prince. In Benares the reception was mixed but the students cheered his attempted speech in Urdu. At Delhi he was cheered by thousands and it was the same in the princely states which received him in courtly splendour as the future Emperor of India. In Gwalior state he was greeted by Maharajah's son and daughter, named respectively George and Mary, after his parents. The Indian army welcomed him with a review and a meeting with some elderly mutiny veterans. Big game hunting was indulged in as only the Indian Princes could provide, with tiger and rhino. At the state of Jodhpur, the Maharajah introduced the Prince to the exciting and dangerous sport of pig sticking. Here in the feudal states the Prince, relaxed and enjoyed the sumptuous hospitality of old India. He paid a week's visit to Burma and then on to Ceylon. From there he travelled to Malaya, Singapore and Hong Kong. After a state visit to Japan, the Prince returned to England after eight months away from home and his family.

EAST AFRICA, 1924 AND 1925

THE DUKE AND DUCHESS OF YORK were married in 1923; the Duke, later George VI, was the second son of King George V. Their first visit to the Empire was in December of 1924 when they toured East Africa. Landing at Mombasa, they went on to Nairobi and then into the interior. They visited Uganda and were entertained by the King. Travel was by car and they lived in tents (*fig. 100*). The Duke indulged in some big game shooting as they moved along. At various places the native tribesmen assembled to pay them homage; at Tonga, for example, 12,000 warriors assembled to dance and give presents to the King's son. They returned to London in April 1925, after a successful tour.

AFRICA, 1925

IN THE SPRING of 1925, the Prince of Wales set out on his last Empire tour, this time to Africa. The first ports of call were the West Coast, Gambia, Sierra Leone, and the Gold Coast. The most important ceremony was the formal reception of the chiefs, and hundreds of African retainers, huge umbrellas and the bright costumes made the sight an unforgettable one (*fig. 105*). The chiefs' costumes were decorated with gold ornaments and some wore crowns of gold as well. Their courtiers were kept busy fanning them with elephant tails. The chiefs presented the Prince with a sword of solid gold, blessed with magic rites and annointed with gin. At Nigeria, the Prince journeyed by train to the north to meet the rulers of the Northern Territories. Here he was met by 20,000 tribesmen on horseback – a spectacle from the Middle Ages – with some wearing chain mail armour and others in leopard skin coats, or turbans and flowing arab clothes. The court jesters, pages, and dancers made it a great and unforgetable occasion. The Prince then returned to the coast and his ship and moved on to Cape Town, South Africa. Enormous crowds were there to greet him and so great was the crowd that they threatened to break through the barriers. Even the nationalists took to him; one prominent politician said, 'Prince we want you to stop here and be our first President'. He travelled 10,000 miles by train, and met 25,000 Boer farmers at Bloemfontein, and addressed them in Afrikaans, much to their delight. The Prince was of course received as the son of the Great White King in tribal areas. The scenes were impressive with huge gatherings of warriors and tribal dancers. He was showered with gifts of weapons and shields, elephant tusks and skins. To meet the proud Zulu warriors the Prince wore the full dress scarlet uniform of the Welsh Guards, with the ribbon of the order of the garter across his chest, and glittering decorations. It was at this time that the Prince celebrated his thirty-first birthday. The tour continued into Bechuanaland and Rhodesia for more tribal gatherings and displays. After a visit to see the Victoria Falls, the Prince returned to South Africa and his ship after one of his most successful tours, having overcome the difficult political situations.

Australia, 1926

In 1926 the Government of Australia invited the Duke and Duchess of York to inaugurate the opening of the federal parliament at the new capital, Canberra. The Royal couple departed in the warship *HMS Renown*, the same warship that had carried his brother, the Prince of Wales, on his own Empire tours. The tour started in New Zealand after the Royal couple had crossed the Pacific, stopping off at Fiji on the way. Their welcome in New Zealand and at Dunedin was tumultuous; the Duke could not make himself heard above the cheering (*fig. 110*). At Rotorua the Maoris gave a demonstration of dances and ceremonies and were unstinting in their welcome. In Australia it was thought that Sydney would be cool in its reception, but the city surpassed itself with its welcome. Hundreds of thousands awaited the Duke and Duchess. Throughout the Australian tour there was no doubt of the peoples' loyalty and affection for the Royal family. The Duke recalled the Australian tour as 'a marvellous exhibition of undisciplined loyalty'. The members of the Royal suite, however, suffered in various ways: one split his trousers in the crush, another found afterwards that the dress studs on his shirt were squashed flat, and another had bruised ribs. From Australia they visited Tasmania, and then back again to mainland of Australia for the inauguration of the new Federal Capital, Canberra. *HMS Renown* steamed homeward stopping off at Western Australia and Mauritius before reaching London in June 1927.

Africa, 1934

The King's fourth son, Prince George Duke of Kent, made a tour of Southern Africa in 1934. He travelled out on the Royal Mail steamship *Caernarvon Castle*, and after landing in South Africa, journeyed north to Southern Rhodesia and eventually to the site of Lusaka, which was about to be built as the capital of Northern Rhodesia. The Duke returned to South Africa and came home on the *Windsor Castle*, a P & O steamship.

AUSTRALIA, 1934

THE KING'S THIRD SON, Prince Henry, Duke of Gloucester, visited Australia in October 1934. Following the success of his elder brother, he also made a call at Tasmania, before reaching New Zealand in January 1935. In the north island the Maoris gave him their traditional friendly welcome to a member of the Royal family. In 1935 the Duke of Kent, now married to Princess Marina of Greece, made a tour of the West Indies. The following year King George V died and his eldest son was proclaimed King Edward VIII. By the time the King had abdicated and his younger brother had been crowned George VI, the war in Europe loomed closer and so the Empire tours ended. After the Second World War the Commonwealth was born, and Royal tours continued as before, to further the personal link between the Throne and the independent nations that formed the Commonwealth with the British Monarch as its head.

— 2 —
ARCH OF WELCOME AT MONTREAL, 1860.
Prince Edward travelled by steamer from Quebec to Montreal where
40,000 people were waiting to greet him, crowding on to the piers and
every vantage point along the route. A great procession was formed,
including Iroquois Indians, which proceeded to the exhibition building
where His Royal Highness opened the show of Canadian products.
The Royal party then carried on to the ceremony at Victoria Bridge.

— 3 —
EDWARD, PRINCE OF WALES, AT THE INAUGURATION OF VICTORIA BRIDGE,
MONTREAL, 25 AUGUST 1860.
The Victoria tubular bridge, which spanned the St Lawrence River,
was one of the great engineering triumphs of the age. The Prince laid
the last stone and clinched the last rivet before declaring the bridge
open. In the evening there were illuminations and fireworks from the
bridge.

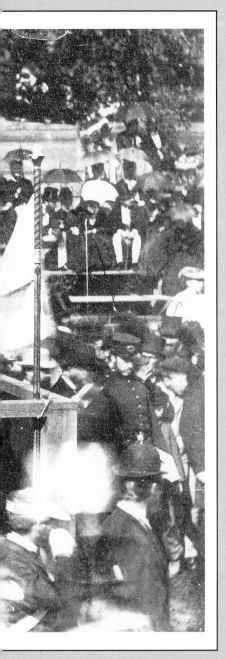

— 4 —
THE PRINCE AND HIS SUITE AT POINT VIEW, NIAGARA FALLS 1860.
The Prince of Wales rested here for four days after the arduous tour of
Quebec, Ottawa, Montreal and Toronto. On 20 September he
proceeded to Detroit and the USA. Prince Edward is the figure in the
centre with his foot on a rock.

— 5 —

RECEPTION OF EDWARD, PRINCE OF WALES, AT NEW YORK, 11 OCTOBER
1860.

The Prince disembarked from the cutter *Harriet Lane* at the battery
and was greeted by the Mayor of New York City, Fernando Wood.
There followed a review of the New York militia and then a parade up
Broadway. Thousands of people lined the route and thronged about
the hotel where the Prince was staying. The next evening the Prince
was fêted at a ball given in his honour at the New York Academy of
Music, where he danced until five in the morning.

— 6 —

THE PRINCE OF WALES AND HIS SUITE, NEW YORK, 1860.
This image was taken at the studio of the famous photographer
Matthew Brady, who was to become well known for his photographs of
the American Civil War that broke out the next year. From left to
right: William Brodie, Major Teasdale, Doctor Ackland (the Prince's
physician), Lieutenant Colonel Gray, Charles Eliot, Lord Lyons (the
British Minister), Lord St Germains, Lord Hinchinbrook, the Prince,
the Duke of Newcastle (Minister for the Colonies), General Bruce (the
Prince's tutor), G.B. Inglehart, G.F. Jenner and Frederick Warre.

— 7 —

THE PRINCE OF WALES IN PORTLAND, MAINE,
20 OCTOBER 1860.
After a visit to Boston the Prince journeyed to
Portland where the Royal squadron lay
anchored. A carriage procession passed
through the thousands of people that lined the
route down to the harbour. Accompanying the
Prince in the carriage is the Duke of
Newcastle, Lord Lyons and Major Howard. It
was from here that the Prince embarked for
the voyage back to Great Britain.

— 8 —

HMS GALATEA, DRESSED OVERALL FOR THE
ARRIVAL IN AUSTRALIA, 1867.
Prince Alfred, Duke of Edinburgh and second
son of Queen Victoria, was the first Royal
visitor to Australia. He made the Royal Navy
his career and it was in his own ship, the
Galatea, that he sailed to Australia and New
Zealand.

— 9 —
PRINCE ALFRED, DUKE OF EDINBURGH, AT GORT HOUSE, TASMANIA,
1867.
Gort House was the Government House of this island and the Prince
was a guest here during his visit.

PRINCE ALFRED, DUKE OF EDINBURGH, KANGAROO HUNTING, 1867.
The colonists brought with them to Australia their love of fox hunting,
but substituted the kangaroo for the fox. It can be seen that dress was
casual. Kangaroos were also hunted at this time with long spears like
pig sticking in India.

— 11 —
PRINCE ALFRED, DUKE OF EDINBURGH, AT LUNCH NEAR LAKE ALBERT,
SOUTH AUSTRALIA, 1867.
This was during the Prince's visit to Campbellhouse sheep station near
Adelaide. The Prince is seated in the centre, using his knife and fork.

— 12 —

PRINCE ALFRED, DUKE OF EDINBURGH, AT ADELAIDE, SOUTH AUSTRALIA,
1867.
The Prince was given a rousing welcome by the Australians on his
arrival and the tour was a great success. The attempted assassination of
the Prince by an Irish Fenian, who shot him in the back only increased
his popularity. He was nursed by one of Florence Nightingale's nurses
who had recently arrived in Australia.

— 13 —
PRINCE ALFRED, DUKE OF EDINBURGH, AT A
GOLD MINE, SOUTH AUSTRALIA, 1867.
Gold had been discovered in 1851 and there
was soon a gold rush to rival that of Calfornia
in the 1840s. There were some dramatic
individual finds: a shepherd uncovered a block
of quartz that yielded 106lb of pure gold. A
single claim yielded £50,000 in eight weeks.

— 14 —
A DECORATED ARCH TO WELCOME PRINCE
ALFRED, DUKE OF EDINBURGH, 1869.
Prince Alfred, the second son of Queen
Victoria, visited New Zealand in 1869; the
tour had been planned for the previous year
but was interrupted by the attempted
assassination of the Prince in Sydney. Fully
recovered, he reached Wellington on 11 April
1869, on board his ship *HMS Galatea*.
Erecting decorated arches was a custom the
English settlers had brought with them and
this one at Lyttelton near Christchurch is
covered in greenery.

— 15 —
CROWDS OUTSIDE THE CLAREDON HOTEL,
CHRISTCHURCH, NEW ZEALAND, 1869.
The colonists came in numbers to see the
Duke of Edinburgh, and can be seen here
hoping to catch a glimpse of Prince Alfred
who was staying at the hotel.

— 16 —
DECORATED ARCH AT QUEEN'S WHARF, WELLINGTON, NEW ZEALAND,
1869.
Prince Alfred, Duke of Edinburgh, had arrived in Lyttelton Harbour
on board his ship *HMS Galatea* and was brought by train to
Christchurch station where a red carpet led to the reception tent. He
was then taken by carriage through the streets filled with cheering
throngs of people.

— 17 —
Kaiapoi Maoris waiting for Prince Alfred, 22 April 1869.
In the garden of Doctor A.C. Barker's house in Christchurch. These
Maoris were dressed in blue coats with scarlet sashes and white
trousers, with feathers in their caps. They numbered about 50 and
camped at North Hagley Park. They marched in the procession
through the city carrying a Union Jack. After the Duke had visited
Dunedin he returned to Wellington, and then on to Auckland for a
protracted stay as it was hoped the Duke's presence might have a
beneficial effect in the stalemate between the Maori king and the
Government. The Prince left for the Fiji Islands on 1 June 1869.

— 18 —
PRINCE ARTHUR, DUKE OF CONNAUGHT AND STRATHEARN, AT BELMERE,
1870.
Prince Arthur was the third son of Queen Victoria and visited Canada
in 1869/70. He was the house guest of Mr Hugh Allen, the financier
and steamship proprietor, who had a country house on Lake
Memphremagog, Quebec Province. The Prince is seated at the table in
a light-coloured suit.

— 19 —
PRINCE ARTHUR, DUKE OF CONNAUGHT AND STRATHEARN, CANADA,
1870.
The Prince and the house party of the financier Hugh Allen are seen
cruising on Lake Memphremagog. The lake is part of the border with
the United States and adjoins Vermont State.

— 20 —

PRINCE ARTHUR, DUKE OF CONNAUGHT AND STRATHEARN, ON THE
VERANDAH OF ARCHIBALD HENDERSON'S HOUSE, 1870.

The Prince addressed the Canadian Militia at the time of the Louis
Riel uprising, which was partly caused by the selling of the Hudson
Bay Company lands to the Dominion of Canada. Prince Arthur is in
the foreground with the paper in his hand; the figure in the frock coat
is Lieutenant General James Lindsay, Commander in Chief. Behind
the General is Colonel Thackman. The other military officers are
Colonel Martindale on the far left, and the young officer at the back is
Captain Fitzgeorge. On the far right is Mr Henderson, Mayor of
Huntingdon.

— 21 —
PRINCE ARTHUR, DUKE OF CONNAUGHT AND STRATHEARN, IN OTTAWA,
1870.
The Prince, who is sitting in the snow second from the left, and a
party of friends are tobogganing in the winter snow. The Prince went
home to marry Princess Louise Margret of Prussia in 1879, but he
returned to Canada in 1911 as Governor General and Commander in
Chief of the Dominion.

— 22 —

EDWARD, PRINCE OF WALES, AND HIS STAFF AT
GOVERNMENT HOUSE, BOMBAY, 8 NOVEMBER
1875.
The Prince landed at Bombay for the start of
his tour of the Indian Empire. With the
Prince is the Viceroy Lord Northbrook, the
Governor of Bombay Province and Major
General Sam Browne, who lost his arm in the
Indian Mutiny of 1857 and also won the
Victoria Cross.

— 23 —

EDWARD, PRINCE OF WALES, AT AGRA, 25
JANUARY 1876.
The Prince and his suite are with Sir John
Strachey, Lieutenant Governor of the North
West Province. It was here that the Prince
visited the Taj Mahal and received the Princes
of the province at a durbar and a procession of
their armed followers. On 31 January the
Prince of Wales left for a visit to the
Maharajah of Gwalior.

— 24 —

EDWARD, PRINCE OF WALES, WITH SIR JUNG
BAHADUR RANA, FEBRUARY 1876.
The Prince of Wales spent from 8 February
until 5 March in Nepal as a guest of the
Maharajah Sir Jung Bahadur Rana who ruled
the country in the place of the King of Nepal.
The Maharajah seized power in 1846 and his
family then ruled Nepal until the King
regained his throne in 1951. Here, the Prince
of Wales hunted big game, elephant and tiger,
for which the state was famous.

— 25 —

PRINCE ALBERT VICTOR, DUKE OF CLARENCE
AND AVONDALE, WITH HIS BROTHER PRINCE
GEORGE OF WALES, IN ADELAIDE, SOUTH
AUSTRALIA, JUNE 1881.

The two sons of Edward, Prince of Wales,
were sent on a world cruise in *HMS
Bacchante*. The two boys held the rank of
midshipmen in the Royal Navy and are
wearing their uniform. The Prince of Wales
had decided that a tour of the Empire would
be more beneficial to the young Princes than
visiting European courts.

— 26 —

PRINCE ALBERT VICTOR, DUKE OF CLARENCE
AND AVONDALE, AND HIS BROTHER, PRINCE
GEORGE OF WALES AT BALLARAT, 1881.

The two Princes visited a gold mine at
Ballarat in the state of Victoria, and wearing
thick canvas trousers and oilskin coats
descended down the shaft. The miners met
them at the 420 feet level by singing the
National Anthem and they then drank their
health. On the right of Prince Albert Victor
stands the Earl of Clanwilliam, Rear Admiral
and Commander of the Squadron. Behind the
head of Prince George is Captain Durrant, of
HMS Cleopatra. Next to him, behind Prince
George, stands Lord Henry Phipps.

— 27 —

PRINCE ALBERT VICTOR, DUKE OF CLARENCE
AND AVONDALE, WITH HIS BROTHER PRINCE
GEORGE AT BRISBANE, AUSTRALIA, 1881.
The two Princes rode through the city in a
procession, and as the Governor had
proclaimed a public holiday crowds of people
turned out to cheer them. The Princes wrote
home 'We have enjoyed ourselves more in
Australia than anywhere since we left
England.'

— 28 —

THE STATE HUT OF THE TWO PRINCES IN FIJI,
1881.
The islands had only come under British rule
six years previously, but the two young
Princes were received with full honour by the
islanders. This hut was constructed in the
grounds of Government House on a platform
of stones and ornamented with intricate forms
of decoration done only for very great chiefs.
Inspired by the example of the islanders,
Prince George decorated his brother's nose
and his own with broad arrows. It was so
realistic that the horrified ship's officers
thought they had been tattooed. Fortunately it
washed off, much to the relief of the captain!

— 29 —
PRINCE ALBERT VICTOR, DUKE OF CLARENCE AND AVONDALE, ARRIVES IN
INDIA, 1889.
The Prince is arriving in Bombay, and is sitting on the right at the
back of the carriage. As the son and heir of the Prince of Wales
(Edward VII) and a future Emperor of India it was considered
essential that the Prince should tour the sub-continent. His recent love
affair with the Catholic Princess Helene of Orleans might also have
been a reason for a Royal tour.

— 30 —

PRINCE ALBERT VICTOR, DUKE OF CLARENCE AND AVONDALE, AT
CALCUTTA, 1889.

The Prince is standing on the steps of Government House in Calcutta,
which at that time was the capital of India. The Prince died in 1892 of
pneumonia, and his younger brother, Prime George, became the heir
to the throne after the Prince of Wales (Edward VII). It was Prince
George who, as George V, moved the capital of India back to Delhi in
1911.

— 31 —

PRINCE ALBERT VICTOR, DUKE OF CLARENCE AND AVONDALE, WITH
LIEUTENANT GENERAL SIR FREDERICK ROBERTS, 1889.
The Prince was visiting the army at Muridke, and is about to ride on
to the parade ground with the General. The Prince is wearing the
uniform of his regiment, the 10th Prince of Wales's own Hussars. The
servant is swatting dust from the glossy patent leather boots. The 10th
Hussars was a very expensive and smart regiment whose Colonel was
the Prince of Wales.

— 32 —
PRINCE ALBERT VICTOR, DUKE OF CLARENCE AND AVONDALE, WITH THE
COMMANDER IN CHIEF'S STAFF, 1889.
Lieutenant General Sir Frederick Roberts was Commander in Chief of
India from 1885 to 1893. He won the Victoria Cross during the Indian
Mutiny of 1857, and carried on to be one of the most successful
generals in India. In 1895 he received the baton of a Field Marshal,
and became Commander in Chief of the British Army in 1901. He
stands just behind his daughter; Lady Roberts sits opposite, with
Prince Albert Victor behind her.

— 33 —
QUEEN STREET ARCH, BRISBANE, QUEENSLAND, 1901.
The Duke and Duchess of Cornwall and York, later George V and
Queen Mary, had arrived in Australia on 6 May 1901 at the start of
their tour of Australia and New Zealand. After opening the Parliament
of the Dominion of Australia, they had journeyed north to Queensland.
The crowds are beginning to gather behind the barriers to watch the
parade. The arch is decorated with electric lights and portraits of the
King and Queen, Edward VII and Queen Alexandra.

— 34 —
THE DUKE AND DUCHESS OF CORNWALL AND YORK IN GEORGE STREET,
BRISBANE, 1901.
The enthusiastic crowds that greeted the Royal couple everywhere can
be seen surrounding the Royal carriage, at the windows and even on
the rooftops. At the side of the carriage rides the Duke's ADC in the
uniform of the Royal Horse Guards. Lining the route are Australian
troops, back from the war in South Africa.

— 35 —
ABORIGINAL DANCERS, BRISBANE, 1901.
Decorated with emu feathers and painted with lines of red and white
ochre on their bodies, the Aborigines danced for the Royal visitors.
The man in front is wearing a kangaroo skin. The spears are over 12
feet high and some of the men are carrying boomerangs.

— 36 —
LANDING PAVILION, SYDNEY HARBOUR 27 MAY 1901.
The Royal yacht entered the harbour at Sydney and anchored in Farm
Cove. Cheering crowds lined the shores as the Royal barge brought the
Duke and Duchess of Cornwall and York to this decorated pavilion. In
the front is the Guard of Honour. From here the Royal visitors were
driven in an open carriage to Government House, which stands above
Farm Cove and commands a splendid view of Sydney.

— 37 —

THE MAYOR OF AUCKLAND PRESENTING AN
ADDRESS TO THE DUKE AND DUCHESS OF
CORNWALL AND YORK, 11 JUNE 1901.
Auckland was the first port of call on the
Royal tour of New Zealand. The Duke and
Duchess arrived by the Orient steamship
Ophir, converted into a Royal yacht for the
tour of the Royal couple. The Mayor of
Auckland, Sir John Logan, is presenting a
loyal address of welcome.

— 38 —

SCHOOL CHILDREN AT AUCKLAND, 11 JUNE
1901.
These schoolchildren formed a living Union
Jack outside the municiple building and
library on the arrival of the Duke and
Duchess. The Duke also laid the foundation
stone of the Victoria School for Maori girls.

— 39 —

HIGHLAND SOLDIERS DRAWN UP AT DUNEDIN FOR THE ROYAL VISIT, JUNE
1901.
The Dunedin Highland Rifles (Volunteers) were formed in 1885, and
wore the tartan of the British 42nd Highland Regiment, the Black
Watch. Three other Scottish volunteer regiments were raised from
colonists from Scotland. These were the Christchurch Highlanders, the
Wanganui Highland Rifles, and the Wellington Highland Rifles. When
the Boer War broke out in 1899, they sent ten contingents which
fought hard and were highly praised.

— 40 —
LAYING THE FOUNDATION STONE FOR THE WELLINGTON TOWN HALL,
JUNE 1901.
The Duke and Duchess of Cornwall and York are in the centre of the
photograph and the Duchess has turned her head towards the camera;
the duke is hidden by the other guests. On the far right with the beard
and wearing a medal is the Prime Minister, the Right Hon,
R.J. Seddon, known as King Dick Seddon. He was the most famous
New Zealand politician.

— 41 —
THE DUKE AND DUCHESS OF CORNWALL AND YORK ARRIVE AT THE
PARLIAMENT BUILDING, WELLINGTON, JUNE 1901.
The Royal carriage has just arrived with the Duke and Duchess, who
are sitting at the back. On the steps in Hussar uniform is the Duchess's
brother, Prince Alexander of Teck. At the top of the steps stands the
Prime Minister, the Rt. Hon. R.J. Seddon. There was at this time a
further presentation of South African war medals from the steps of the
Parliament Building.

— 42 —
GROUP OF SCHOOLGIRLS WAITING TO PRESENT BOUQUETS TO THE DUCHESS
OF CORNWALL AND YORK FROM THE CHILDREN OF CANTERBURY, JUNE
1901.
These demure young ladies represented the 80 schools of the area.
Over 8000 schoolchildren gathered to greet the Royal party. As the
Royal carriage bearing the Duke and Duchess arrived all the children
united in singing the National Anthem.

— 43 —
PRINCE GEORGE, DUKE OF CORNWALL AND YORK, MEETING MILITARY
VETERANS, 24 JUNE 1901.
These are veterans of the Maori wars of New Zealand which were
caused by the desire of the colonists for increasing amounts of land.
The Maoris complained that they had been told by the missionaries to
look up to heaven for salvation, but while they did this the white men
had stolen the land from under their feet. The officer on the far left of
the Duke in the Hussar uniform is Prince Alexander of Teck, ADC to
the Duke and his brother-in-law.

— 44 —
PRINCE GEORGE, DUKE OF CORNWALL AND YORK, PRESENTING
DECORATIONS, 24 JUNE 1901.
The Prince is presenting medals and decorations to members of the
New Zealand forces returning from the war in South Africa at the
military review at Hagley Park Christchurch. The officer in the
uniform of the Royal Horse Guards is Viscount Crichton, ADC to the
Prince.

— 45 —
THE MILITARY REVIEW AT HAGLEY PARK, 24
JUNE 1901.
The Militia Act of 1858 gave the Government
the right to raise volunteers, as distinct from
militia, in order to preserve the peace within
the colony. Volunteers were used in the later
part of the nineteenth century against the
Maoris. They also fought in the South African
War, from which they had recently returned
when this review took place. On this occasion
the Prince wore the uniform of Colonel of the
City of London Regiment, the Royal Fusiliers.

— 46 —

THE DUKE AND DUCHESS OF CORNWALL AND
YORK AT DUNEDIN, 1901.
The guard of honour at the back is in the
'Present Arms' position and are from the
Otago Rifle Volunteers, which had fought in
South Africa. The banner in the background
is for the Orangemen organization. From
Dunedin the Royal couple left New Zealand
for Tasmania.

— 47 —

THE DUKE AND DUCHESS OF CORNWALL AND
YORK AT HOBART, TASMANIA, 1901.
As the second part of their tour of Australia
began the Duke and Duchess called at the
island of Tasmania, part of the Dominion of
Australia but fiercely independent. Riding at
the side of the carriage is the Duke's ADC
and friend, the Viscount Crichton.

— 48 —

REVIEW OF TASMANIAN VOLUNTEERS, HOBART,
TASMANIA, 1901.
One of the duties of the Duke and Duchess
was to lay the foundation stone of the
Tasmanian Soldiers' Monument, a memorial
to their comrades sleeping on the battlefields
of South Africa. Nearly 600 Tasmanians had
gone to fight the Boers: two had won the
supreme accolade, the Victoria Cross, and 15
had died in the field.

— 49 —
TRIUMPHAL ARCH, HOBART, TASMANIA, 1901.
One of several elaborate arches erected to celebrate the visit of the
Duke and Duchess of Cornwall and York. This particular arch was
manufactured by the Marine Board of Hobart, and although it looks
solid, it is only lightly constructed of wood with painted decoration.
Other arches were erected in Hobart, including one by the apple
growers which was covered in apples, and another made of barrels in
the harbour area.

— 50 —
THE DUKE AND DUCHESS OF CORNWALL AND YORK AT ADELAIDE, SOUTH
AUSTRALIA, 1901.
The procession is near the gates of Government House, Adelaide.
Great crowds turned out to see the Royal couple as in the other cities
of Australia. The Duke had been here in 1881 with his elder brother,
the Duke of Clarence and Avondale, when they were on their world
tour.

— 51 —
LAYING THE FOUNDATION STONE OF THE QUEEN'S HOME HOSPITAL,
ADELAIDE, 1901.
The Duke and Duchess laid the foundation stone on July 1901. It is
now known as the Queen Victoria Maternity Hospital. The Royal
couple can be seen in the centre of the photograph walking towards the
foundation stone. The flag-waving schoolchildren have pressed
forward to see them. In the background is an escort of South
Australian Mounted Rifles.

— 52 —
ROYAL PROCESSION IN KING WILLIAM STREET, ADELAIDE, 1901.
The Royal carriage with its escort of mounted Volunteers is passing
down King William Street. Lining the route are soldiers from the
South Australian Scottish Regiment, which had sent volunteers to
South Africa in the late Boer War.

— 53 —

THE DUKE AND DUCHESS OF CORNWALL AND YORK AT GLENELG, SOUTH AUSTRALIA, 1901. From Adelaide to Perth in Western Australia the Royal couple travelled by train. On 15 July they were at Glenelg to meet the local dignitaries and sign the visitors' book. In the background can be seen the typical towns of outback Australia, with their covered shops to protect the passing shoppers.

— 54 —

UNVEILING THE STATUE OF QUEEN VICTORIA, 21 SEPTEMBER 1901. As part of the Duke and Duchess of Cornwall and York's duties at Ottawa, there was an unveiling of a statue of the late Queen Victoria, the Duke's grandmother. A party of soldiers from a Canadian Fusilier Regiment is drawn up awaiting the arrival of the Royal party. In the background are the Parliament buildings for which his father, when Prince of Wales, had laid the foundation stone in 1860.

— 55 —
THE DUKE AND DUCHESS OF CORNWALL AND
YORK AT ROCKCLIFFE PARK.
To reach the park the Royal couple travelled
by the Ottawa electric railway car which can
be seen in the background. The Duke is to the
centre left holding on to his hat; the Duchess
is in front wearing a white dress.

— 56 —
SHOOTING THE RAPIDS AT OTTAWA, 1901.
Lumber is one of the industries of Ottawa and
on their tour of the city the Duke and
Duchess were invited by the lumbermen to
shoot the rapids on a timber raft. They did
this following the example of the King who
had shot the rapids on his 1860 tour of
Canada.

— 57 —
INDIAN WARRIOR AWAITING THE ARRIVAL OF
THE ROYAL TRAIN, SEPTEMBER 1901.
A warrior of the Siksika tribe, commonly
known as the Blackfeet because of their black
dyed moccasins. The Siksika tribe ranged over
this part of Canada as well as the USA. They
used to be at war with all the neighbouring
Indians but they were on relatively friendly
terms with the English whom they depended
for guns and ammunition.

— 58 —
INDIAN CAMP AT SHAGANNAPI POINT NEAR CALGARY, 1901.
This camp, which was erected by the Indians awaiting the arrival of
the Duke and Duchess of Cornwall and York, displays several types of
tent. The teepees made of buffalo hide were now replaced by canvas
but made in the traditional manner. Others used the army pattern tents
bought in trade.

— 59 —
CALGARY RAILWAY STATION, 1901.
Waiting at the station for the Duke and Duchess of Cornwall and York
is a troop of Royal Canadian Mounted Police, and the dog that
invariably appears on these occasions. The carriages drawn up on the
left are for the Royal party.

— 60 —
MOUNTED ESCORT, CALGARY, 1901.
A squadron of Royal Canadian Mounted
Police escort the Duke of Cornwall and York,
who can be seen on the left of the picture in
the Fusilier bearskin headress with his ADCs.
The uniform at this time was the familiar red
coat, white pith helmet, and dark blue
breeches, and they were armed with carbines.
Pay was a dollar a day, all found.

— 61 —

THE DUKE AND DUCHESS OF CORNWALL AND
YORK AT CALGARY, 30 SEPTEMBER 1901.
The Royal party are welcomed at the entrance
to the court house. Down the street can be
seen the Dominion of Canada assay office.
The mounted troops are drawn from the
Royal Canadian Mounted Police and the foot
guard of honour is from the 6th regiment, the
Duke of Connaught's own rifles.

— 62 —

THE DUKE AND DUCHESS OF CORNWALL AND
YORK AT A MEETING WITH THE INDIAN CHIEF'S,
CALGARY, 1901.
A host of red indian tribesmen came out to see
and meet the Royal visitors the Duke was,
after all, the grandson of the Great White
Mother. The tribes included Blackfoot, Blood,
Sarcee, Piegan, and Stoney Cree Indians.
Drawn up on this side are a line of Royal
Canadian Mounted Police.

— 63 —
THE ROYAL TRAIN ARRIVES AT VANCOUVER, BRITISH COLOMBIA, 1901.
The Royal tour of Canada was made by Canadian Pacific Railway; this
allowed the Duke and Duchess to travel the length of the Dominion in
comfort and in a reasonable time. They were accompanied by the
Prime Minister of Canada, Sir Wilfred Laurier, a French-Canadian.
As Vancouver is on the western seaboard the guard of honour was
drawn from the Royal Canadian Navy.

— 64 —
RECEPTION OF THE DUKE AND DUCHESS OF CORNWALL AND YORK AT
HALIFAX, NOVIA SCOTIA, 19 OCTOBER 1901.
This was at the conclusion of the Canadian tour of the Duke and
Duchess. The Royal party then left for St John's Newfoundland where
the steamship *Ophir* lay, ready to carry them back to Great Britain.
They arrived at Portsmouth on 30 October 1901.

— 65 —
THE PRINCE AND PRINCESS OF WALES, LATER GEORGE V AND QUEEN
MARY, 9 NOVEMBER 1905.
Arriving on *HMS Renown* the Royal couple were given a rousing
welcome at Bombay, their first step on Indian soil. The Prince read an
address to the city of Bombay expressing his delight to be in India and
to thank the city for its loyal devotion to his father, the King Emperor.
Included in this group on the dais is the Viceroy and Vicereine, Lord
and Lady Curzon. The building to the front is the Royal Bombay
Yacht Club.

— 66 —
THE PRINCE OF WALES TIGER SHOOTING IN JAIPUR, NOVEMBER, 1905.
The Maharajah of Jaipur was able to supply his Royal guest with some
excellent big game shooting. This was the first tiger the Prince had
shot and was over nine feet long. It was killed by one bullet at 120
yards as it ran towards the Prince.

— 67 —
THE PRINCE AND PRINCESS OF WALES AT UDAIPUR, 18 NOVEMBER 1905.
The Royal couple are seen here arriving at the Maharajah of Udaipur's
palace. The Maharajah ruled a state in Rajputana of over 12,000 square
miles, and was regarded by his Hindu subjects as a direct descendant
of the god Rama. A durbar was held at the palace for the nobles of the
state to meet the Prince and Princess; they also swore allegiance to
their King Emperor.

— 68
THE PRINCE OF WALES DECORATING INDIAN ARMY OFFICERS IN LAHORE,
DECEMBER 1905.
The Prince of Wales inspected the Imperial Service Troops of the
Punjab at Mian Mir Parade Ground in Lahore. These were troops of
the native Indian states and had been trained and improved to be fit to
take their place in the field should the need arise.

— 69 —
THE PRINCE AND PRINCESS OF WALES WITH THE COMMANDER IN CHIEF
OF INDIA, 1 DECEMBER 1905.
The Commander in Chief was General the Viscount Kitchener of
Khartoum, and it was here at Kala Serai that the Prince of Wales
reviewed the Indian Army – a force of 100,000 men. Army manoeuvres
were held and among the guests was General MacArthur of the United
States.

— 70 —
THE STATE ENTRY INTO GWALIOR, 20 DECEMBER 1905.
Thirty-six regal elephants carried the Maharajah Scindia of Gwalior
and his Royal guests to the palace. In the elephants' ears were earings
of gold, and solid silver chains ringed their ankles. The heavily
embroidered cloths were decorated with silver bells. It was here the
Prince and Princess of Wales spent Christmas with the Maharajah and
his family.

— 71 —

THE GREAT FORTRESS AT GWALIOR,
DECEMBER 1905.
On Sunday afternoon the Prince and
Princess visited the famous fortress
that had played so conspicuous a
part in the history of Central India.
It is a vast mass of ochreous
sandstone a mile and a half long,
and in places 342 feet high. The
fortress was repaired in 1881.
Having reached the base of the
citadel by motor car the Royal party
continued by stately elephant,
accompanied by their royal host.

— 72 —
CAPTURING WILD ELEPHANTS, MYSORE, JANUARY 1906.
As guests of the Maharajah of Mysore, the Prince and Princess of
Wales witnessed the spectacle of hunting and capturing wild elephants.
The method was to enclose 50 acres of jungle and clear paths through
the jungle towards the *keddah* (corral); a herd of elephants was already
marked down if it was in a 15 mile radius. The elephants were then
driven to the corral by beaters. Once inside the *kumki* (trained
elephants) were introduced to calm down the herd and allow them to
be roped.

— 73 —
THE PRINCE AND PRINCESS OF WALES WITH THE MAHARAJAH OF
BENARES, FEBRUARY 1906.
The Maharajah stands on the right next to the Prince of Wales and
kneeling at the front are his two sons. Once the size of Hyderabad,
Benares was weakened by Warren Hastings at the end of the
eighteenth century; the Maharajah fled to Gwalior and the dynasty
ended. An adopted son was chosen as head of the family to rule a
much smaller and powerless state but they also lost the sovereignty of
the city of Benares. These rights were restored in 1911.

— 74 —
THE ARRIVAL AT HYDERABAD, 8 FEBRUARY 1906.
The Prince of Wales is in the carriage with the Nizam of Hyderabad as
they drive into Hyderabad city to the Royal palace. The Princess of
Wales followed in a second carriage with the British Resident. The
postilions are in the state livery of blue and yellow, which matched the
colour of the Nizam's carriage.

THE PRINCE OF WALES SHOOTING IN HYDERABAD, FEBRUARY 1906.
The leopard, the Prince's first bag of the day, was shot at 60 yards,
between the ears. The tiger, over nine feet long, was shot as it sprung
towards the Prince from a bank; it was hit by one shot behind the
shoulder – an instant kill. The Princess of Wales did not accompany
the Prince but remained at the Falaknama Palace.

— 76 —
THE PRINCESS OF WALES BIDS FAREWELL TO THE NIZAM OF HYDERABAD,
FEBRUARY 1906.
His Highness Mir Mahub Ali Khan, Nizam of Hyderabad, ruled a
Muslim state larger in size than France. His family had seized power
from the Moghul rulers of India in 1723. His income at this time was
six million pounds per year.

ON BOARD THE ROYAL YACHT, THE P & O STEAMER *Medina*, 1911.
The King Emperor George V and Queen Empress Mary are very
much amused by the sailors of the Royal yacht pillow fighting on a
greased mast. On the right is the Queen Empress and her companions:
the Duchess of Devonshire (Mistress of the Robes), and the Countess
of Shaftesbury (Mistress of the Bedchamber). With the King Emperor
stands Sir Derek Keppel, (Master of the Household), the Marquess of
Crewe, (Minister in Attendance), and the Earl of Durham (the Lord
High Steward).

— 78 —
KING GEORGE V AND QUEEN MARY AT DELHI, NOVEMBER 1911.
The King Emperor is wearing the uniform of a British Field Marshal for the state entry into Delhi. Ancient precedent determined that he should use the Delhi gateway opened only when an Emperor was to pass through. The Indian people, however, failed to recognize their Emperor on this occasion because he was dressed in military uniform similar to the other officers in his suite.

— 79 —
KING GEORGE V AND QUEEN MARY LEAVE FOR THEIR CORONATION DURBAR, 12 DECEMBER 1911.
The durbar took place at noon under the fierce Indian sun. The King Emperor and Queen Empress wore full ceremonial robes of velvet and ermine, as well as their crowns. The King Emperor's crown was made up of 6000 diamonds, 4 large sapphires, 4 rubies and 9 emeralds. It was made in London by the court jewellers, Garrards.

— 80 —

THE DURBAR AMPHITHEATRE AT DELHI, 12
DECEMBER 1911.
Under this covered dais sat the Emperor and
Empress of India. Seated on thrones of solid
silver and carpets of cloth of gold, they
received the Princes of India, who swore their
allegience to the Emperor. This was a survival
of the courts of the Moghul Emperors before
the days of British rule. Over 50,000 people
attended as spectators, and the total
participants were estimated at some 100,000
people.

— 81 —

THE KING EMPEROR GEORGE V AND THE
QUEEN EMPRESS MARY AT THE RED FORT
DELHI, 13 DECEMBER 1911.
It was the custom of the Moghul Emperors of
India to show themselves to their people from
the walls of the Red Fort at Delhi and George
V carried on this tradition. The pages of
honour were all young Maharajahs or the sons
of Maharajahs, dressed in white and gold silk
garments and turbans of gold embroidered
silk. This was the day after the coronation
durbar at a garden party given by Their
Majesties in the grounds of Shah Jehan's
Palace at the Red Fort.

— 82 —

KING EMPEROR GEORGE V TIGER SHOOTING IN
NEPAL, 1911.

Ten days after the coronation durbar, the
King Emperor left for two weeks shooting in
Nepal. Queen Mary did not accompany him
but travelled to Agra and Rajputana instead.
The King Emperor, one of the best shots in
Europe, bagged 24 tigers out of a total 39.

— 83 —

THE KING EMPEROR GEORGE V AND THE
VICEROY OF INDIA AT CALCUTTA, 30 DECEMBER
1911.

After the Royal party had left Nepal they
journeyed south by rail to Calcutta and the
Queen Empress rejoined her husband at
Bankipore. A proclamation parade was held in
Calcutta, as well as a review of the army.

— 84 —

THE KING EMPEROR GEORGE V AND QUEEN
EMPRESS MARY DEPART FROM BOMBAY, 10
JANUARY 1812

Two months from the day that they had set
out from Portsmouth the Royal couple
embarked for England. George V was the first
English king to journey beyond Europe since
Richard the Lionheart and the first British
ruler to set foot on Indian soil as sovereign.

— 85 —
EDWARD, PRINCE OF WALES, AT A RELAXED
MOMENT, HALIFAX, NOVIA SCOTIA, 1919.
At the start of his tour of Canada the Prince
said, 'I want Canada to look upon me as a
Canadian, if not actually by birth, yet
certainly in mind and spirit'. Crowds of
thousands of people met him everywhere,
tugging at the buttons on his coat or snatching
at his handkerchief in their enthusiasm.

— 86 —
PRESENTING COLOURS TO THE ST JOHN
FUSILERS, AT ST JOHN, NEW BRUNSWICK, 28
AUGUST 1919.
Raised in 1869 and disbanded in 1871, the
regiment was reactivated in 1872. It
contributed volunteers to the Canadian
Expeditionary Force in 1910 and were
particulary remembered for their actions at
the battle of Ypres in 1917.

— 87 —

EDWARD, PRINCE OF WALES, TROUT FISHING AT
LAKE NIPIGON, ONTARIO, SEPTEMBER 1919.
After the Prince had completed the first part
of his tour he spent a few days' fishing on the
Nipigon. The Prince's staff were left behind
and, accompanied only by a few friends and
indian guides, the Prince journeyed by canoe,
camping on the banks by night.

— 88 —

THE PRINCE OF WALES ADDRESSING THE INDIAN
TRIBES AT BANFF, 17 SEPTEMBER 1919.
At an encampment the Stoney Indians were
waiting in tribal assembly to receive him.
They presented the Prince with a buckskin
robe and a feathered headdress and announced
that he had been elected Tribal Chief, with
the title Morning Star. He immediately
donned the headdress to the delight of the
tribe and made his reply to their address.

— 89 —

EDWARD, PRINCE OF WALES, ARRIVES AT
REGINA, 1919.
The Prince's carriage is escorted by a troop of
Royal Canadian Mounted Police in a formal
parade through the city. He had travelled
across Canada by train as his parents had done
in 1901. At every stop, however, he had made
a speech and even got down on the track to
talk to the farm hands, miners, and workers as
no Prince had ever done before.

— 90 —

EDWARD, PRINCE OF WALES, MEETING THE OFFICERS DURING HIS VISIT TO
THE BARRACKS AT REGINA, 1919.
At the headquarters of the Royal Canadian Mounted Police the Prince
toured the headquarters and was introduced to the officers on the staff.
Here, he is shaking hands with Inspector C.J. Prime and behind the
Prince stands Commissioner A.B. Perry. The other officers are on the
Prince's staff and are Vice-Admiral Halsey, Major General Sir
H. Birstall, and Brigadier Alex Ross.

— 91 —
THE PRINCE OF WALES INSPECTING A MOUNTED TROOP OF THE ROYAL
CANADIAN MOUNTED POLICE, REGINA, 1919.
These troopers had kept law and order on the plains since 1873 – a
total of 300 men to police 300,000 square miles. They are wearing the
very familiar scarlet coat, and the Montana hat. Arms consisted of a
revolver and the carbine kept on the saddle.

— 92 —
THE PRINCE OF WALES INSPECTING DISMOUNTED TROOPERS, REGINA,
1919.
These Mounties, as they were soon nicknamed, were all volunteers.
The original recruiting posters called for young men able to ride, able
bodied and of good character, between the ages of 18 and 40.
Constables' pay was a dollar a day, and, after three years service they
could claim a land grant of 160 acres in the North West Territory.

— 93 —
A ROUGH RIDER DEMONSTRATING HIS MOUNT, REGINA, 1919.
The Prince of Wales was entertained by a display of horsemanship by
the Mounties at their headquarter barracks at Regina. The roughrider,
identified by the spur above the stripes on his right arm, has his foot
on the saddle. It was his task to teach the men to ride in a military
fashion; he also broke in the mustangs bought only half trained. Two
men on his right carry cameras to record the occasion.

THE PRINCE OF WALES'S RECEPTION AT TIMMINS, 16 OCTOBER 1919.
The people of Canada were forthright in their welcome of the Prince;
he, in his turn, went out of his way to meet the man in the street.
Beneath the dignity of a Royal Prince they found a youthful, lively
young man who was a true king of the people. Everywhere they
queued to shake him by the hand – 'put it right here,' said a war
veteran. 'I shook hands with your grandfather.'

— 95 —
THE PRINCE OF WALES AT WEST POINT MILITARY ACADEMY, NOVEMBER
1919.
From Canada the Prince at his own request had visited the USA for
ten days. His reception everywhere was rapturous; New York gave him
a ticker tape welcome; he was met by the President, and attended a
magnificent ball given in his honour. He later visited West Point
Military Academy to inspect the cadets, with Brigadier General
Douglas MacArthur who was Superintendent at that time.

— 96 —

EDWARD, PRINCE OF WALES, AT ROTORUA, NEW ZEALAND, 1920.
The Prince toured New Zealand in April of 1920 and reached Rotorua
on 27 April. Here, there was a great ceremonial gathering of 5000
Maoris. Thirty tribes had assembled under the coordination of Sir
Apirana Ngata who was a political leader of the Maoris in the 1920s.
The Prince is in the uniform of the Welsh Guards and has a Maori
cloak draped over his shoulders; he carries in his hand a *taiha*, the staff
of office of a chieftain.

— 97 —
EDWARD, PRINCE OF WALES, DRIVING THROUGH DUNEDIN, NEW
ZEALAND, 1920.
Dunedin was reached by train on 17 May and the Prince was
accommodated at the Grand Hotel. Huge crowds attended wherever
the Prince was to be seen. Here the motorcade has reached Prince's
Street, Octagon Corner, Dunedin. On 22 May the Prince left on *HMS
Renown* for Australia.

— 98 —
THE PRINCE OF WALES AT THE ROYAL AUSTRALIAN SHOW, 1920.
The Prince of Wales was a good judge of horses and also ran his own
cattle ranch in Canada. Here he is admiring some prize draft horses.
Australia was an arduous assignment for the Prince but his personality
quickly made him popular with the people. He made so many speeches
that he lost his voice by the time the tour reached Tasmania.

— 99 —
THE PRINCE OF WALES ARRIVING AT PERTH, WESTERN AUSTRALIA, 1920.
Prince Edward was only 26 at the time of his Australian tour, yet he
was already a seasoned traveller around the Empire. He had been sent
on a gruelling tour of Canada in 1919, followed by the unique
experience of the trip to the USA. He left Australia, 'half killed by
kindess' and physically exhausted.

— 100 —
THE DUKE AND DUCHESS OF YORK, LATER
GEORGE VI AND QUEEN ELIZABETH, WITH
THEIR AID, EAST AFRICA, 1924.
The Royal couple visited the East African
colonies of Kenya and Uganda in 1924. They
landed at Mombasa and then travelled
overland by Ford motor cars, living under
canvas. They reached Lake Nyasa and Lake
Albert, then lived on a steamer on the White
Nile for five weeks reaching Khartoum in
March 1925.

— 101 —
THE DUKE AND DUCHESS OF YORK WITH THE
KABAKA OF BUGANDA, 1924.
As part of their East African tour, the Duke
and Duchess of York were recieved by the
Kabaka Daudi Chwa II. The Kabaka had
succeeded in 1897 on the deposition of his
father. Buganda was one of the four kingdoms
that made up the colony of Uganda, the others
being Ankole, Bunyoro Kitara and Toro.

— 102 —
THE DUKE AND DUCHESS OF YORK AT A TRIBAL
GATHERING, BUGANDA, 1924.
The Duke sits in the centre, on his right is the
Kabaka Daudi Chwa II and next to him is the
Queen of Buganda, Irene Namaganda. The
Duchess of York sits on the far right of the
picture. The leopard skins are a sign of
kingship, and the Royal party are watching a
display of dancing.

— 103 —
THE DUKE AND DUCHESS OF YORK AT CAMP IN KENYA, 1924.
After the First World War, safaris by motor car became more common
on the open plains of East Africa. The Duke and Duchess of York
decided to use this mode of travel for their safari of 1924. The camera
on the table was more common than the rifle in this part of the world.

— 104 —
THE DUCHESS OF YORK AND HER GUN BEARER, EAST AFRICA, 1924.
Lady Elizabeth Bowes-Lyon, daughter of the 14th Earl of Strathmore
and Kinghorne, had married Prince George, Duke of York, in 1923.
The Duchess sits by her trophy which is a Uganda Kob, common in
East Africa from Kavirondo to Uganda. The horns on this specimen
are particulary fine.

— 105 —
EDWARD, PRINCE OF WALES, AT FREETOWN,
SIERRA LEONE, 1925.
The Prince of Wales received the paramount
chiefs of the country, upon each of whom he
bestowed a medal from the King. There was a
display of native dancing in his honour which
included the girl in the photograph, famous in
Sierra Leone.

— 106 —
EDWARD, PRINCE OF WALES AT A GARDEN
PARTY, SIERRA LEONE, 1925.
The Prince is relaxing with a cup of tea at the
civic garden party, given in his honour at
Victoria Park, Freetown. Once known as the
white man's grave because of the fever-
infested forests and swamps it was now
becoming a modern colony with commercial
prospects.

— 107 —
EDWARD, PRINCE OF WALES, AT THE
AGRICULTURAL SHOW, SIERRA LEONE, 1925.
The Prince toured the exhibition with the
Governor of Sierra Leone, who is seen on his
right. Also on the right stands a boy scout.
The scout movement had spread rapidly
throughout the Empire and had received the
patronage and interest of the Prince's younger
brother, the Duke of York.

— 108 —
EDWARD, PRINCE OF WALES, AT
JOHANNESBURG, JULY 1925.
The Prince of Wales with the Lord Mayor of
Johannesburg receives an address of welcome.
It was feared that because of the political
situation the Prince would not be well
received; however, thousands lined the streets
and the reception was overwhelming. One
Boer politician put his arm around the Prince
and said, 'Prince, we want you to stop here
and be our first president'.

— 109 —

CIVIC RECEPTION AT WELLINGTON FOR THE
DUKE AND DUCHESS OF YORK, 5 MARCH, 1927.
Prince Albert, Duke of York, later to succeed
as George VI, visited New Zealand in 1927
with his wife, the former Lady Elizabeth
Bowes-Lyon. Wellington was reached on 5
March after visits to most of the main towns
of the north island. They are seen here at a
civic reception at the town hall; the Duke is
wearing the uniform of a captain in the Royal
Navy.

— 110 —

THE DUKE AND DUCHESS OF YORK AT NELSON,
NEW ZEALAND, MARCH 1927.
The future George VI and his wife are
walking through lines of school children who
had gathered for the occasion. Walking by the
side of the very elegant and fashionable
Duchess is the Mayor of Nelson. Prince
Albert, Duke of York, is walking behind. It
was here that the Duchess became ill with
tonsilitis and the Duke had to continue the
tour on his own. They met up together at
Bluff on 22 March and then the Royal party
boarded the warship *HMS Renown*.

ACKNOWLEDGMENTS

The author and publisher would like to thank the following for permission to reproduce photographs: HM the Queen: 1, 10–13, 22–4, 27–32; Notman Archives, Canada: 2–3, 21, 57–8, 63; Public Archives of Canada: 4, 18–20, 54–56, 87–88, 94; Library of Congress, USA: 5–8; Tasmanian Archives: 9, 47–9; Auckland Public Library: 14, 37–8 96; Canterbury Museum: 15–17, 42–5, 109–10; The Royal Commonwealth Society: 33–5, 65–80, 82–4, 100–4; Archives of New South Wales, Australia: 36; Otago Early Settlers Museum, New Zealand: 39, 46, 97; Wellington Public Library: 40; New Plymouth City Council: 41; Mortlock Library of South Australia: 50–3; Royal Canadian Mounted Police: 59–62, 89–93; Public Archives of Novia Scotia: 64, 85; The BBC Hulton Picture Library: 86, 98–99, 105–8; West Point Military Academy: 95. All other photographs come from the author and the Batsford archives.